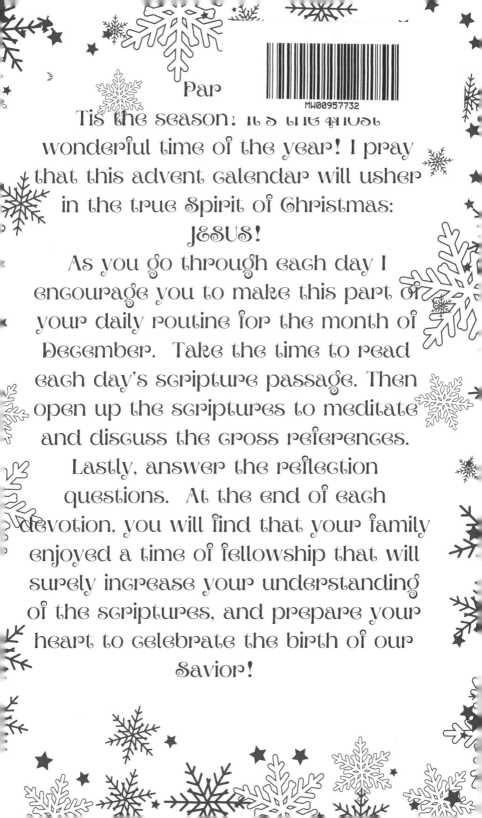

Par

Tis the season! It's the most
wonderful time of the year! I pray
that this advent calendar will usher
in the true Spirit of Christmas:
JESUS!

As you go through each day I
encourage you to make this part of
your daily routine for the month of
December. Take the time to read
each day's scripture passage. Then
open up the scriptures to meditate
and discuss the cross references.

Lastly, answer the reflection
questions. At the end of each
devotion, you will find that your family
enjoyed a time of fellowship that will
surely increase your understanding
of the scriptures, and prepare your
heart to celebrate the birth of our
Savior!

LUKE 1:5-7

There was in the days of Herod, the king of Judea, a certain priest named Zacharias, of the division of Abijah. His wife was of the daughters of Aaron, and her name was Elizabeth. And they were both righteous before God, walking in all the commandments and ordinances of the Lord blameless. But they had no child, because Elizabeth was barren, and they were both well advanced in years.

Cross references Gen. 18:1-15, Luke 1:37

Are you waiting on the Lord for something?

LUKE 1:8-10

So it was, that while he was serving as priest before God in the order of his division, according to the custom of the priesthood, his lot fell to burn incense when he went into the temple of the Lord. And the whole multitude of the people was praying outside at the hour of incense.

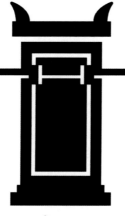

How can you serve the Lord?

cross references: Hebrews 13:15, Rev. 5:10

LUKE 1:11-13

Then an angel of the Lord appeared to him, standing on the right side of the altar of incense. And when Zacharias saw him, he was troubled, and fear fell upon him. But the angel said to him, "Do not be afraid, Zacharias, for your prayer is heard; and your wife Elizabeth will bear you a son, and you shall call his name John.

When has God answered your prayer?

Cross reference
Judges 13:1-24

LUKE 1:14-17

And you will have joy and gladness, and many will rejoice at his birth. For he will be great in the sight of the Lord, and shall drink neither wine nor strong drink. He will also be filled with the Holy Spirit, even from his mother's womb. And he will turn many of the children of Israel to the Lord their God. He will also go before Him in the spirit and power of Elijah, 'to turn the hearts of the fathers to the children,' and the disobedient to the wisdom of the just, to make ready a people prepared for the Lord."

Does God want to use you to turn the hearts of people to God?

cross references Malachi 4:5,6, Mark 9:11-13

LUKE 1:18-20

And Zacharias said to the angel, "How shall I know this? For I am an old man, and my wife is well advanced in years." And the angel answered and said to him, "I am Gabriel, who stands in the presence of God, and was sent to speak to you and bring you these glad tidings. But behold, you will be mute and not able to speak until the day these things take place, because you did not believe my words which will be fulfilled in their own time."

Do you believe God's promises?

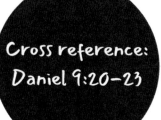

Cross reference: Daniel 9:20-23

LUKE 1:21-23

And the people waited for Zacharias, and marveled that he lingered so long in the temple. But when he came out, he could not speak to them; and they perceived that he had seen a vision in the temple, for he beckoned to them and remained speechless. So it was, as soon as the days of his service were completed, that he departed to his own house.

What has God done that caused you to marvel?

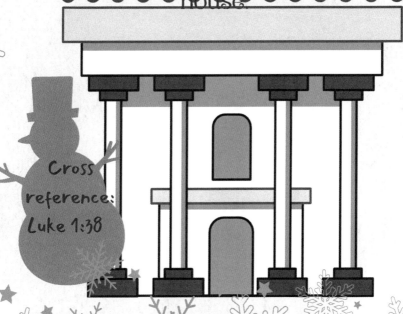

Cross reference: Luke 1:38

LUKE 1:24-25

Now after those days his wife Elizabeth conceived; and she hid herself five months, saying, "Thus the Lord has dealt with me, in the days when He looked on me, to take away my reproach among people."

How has God taken away your reproach of sin?

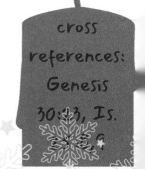

cross references: Genesis 30:23, Is. 6

Luke 1:26-29

Now in the sixth month the angel Gabriel was sent by God to a city of Galilee named Nazareth, to a virgin betrothed to a man whose name was Joseph, of the house of David. The virgin's name was Mary. And having come in, the angel said to her, "Rejoice, highly favored one, the Lord is with you; blessed are you among women!" But when she saw him, she was troubled at his saying, and considered what manner of greeting this was.

Cross references:
Prov. 3:1-4,
Joshua 1:5

what does God say about you?

Then the angel said to her, "Do not be afraid, Mary, for you have found favor with God. And behold, you will conceive in your womb and bring forth a Son, and shall call His name JESUS. He will be great, and will be called the Son of the Highest; and the Lord God will give Him the throne of His father David. And He will reign over the house of Jacob forever, and of His kingdom there will be no end."

Why do you need to not be afraid?

cross references:
Is. 9:7, Is. 7:14

Then Mary said to the angel, "How can this be, since I do not know a man?" And the angel answered and said to her, "The Holy Spirit will come upon you, and the power of the Highest will overshadow you; therefore, also, that Holy One who is to be born will be called the Son of God.

Can you believe God even when you don't understand?

Cross references:
Ps. 2:7,
Acts 8:37
Rom. 1:1-4

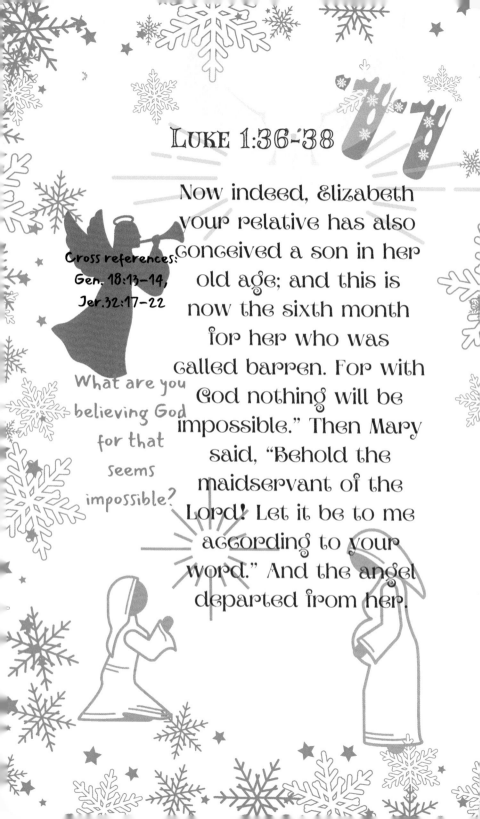

Luke 1:36-38

Now indeed, Elizabeth your relative has also conceived a son in her old age; and this is now the sixth month for her who was called barren. For with God nothing will be impossible." Then Mary said, "Behold the maidservant of the Lord! Let it be to me according to your word." And the angel departed from her.

Cross references: Gen. 18:13-14, Jer. 32:17-22

What are you believing God for that seems impossible?

LUKE 1:39-41

Now Mary arose in those days and went into the hill country with haste, to a city of Judah, and entered the house of Zacharias and greeted Elizabeth. And it happened, when Elizabeth heard the greeting of Mary, that the babe leaped in her womb; and Elizabeth was filled with the Holy Spirit.

Are you filled with the Holy Spirit?

Cross references:
Acts 4:8-12
Acts 13:49-52

LUKE 1:42-45

Then she spoke out with a loud voice and said, "Blessed are you among women, and blessed is the fruit of your womb! But why is this granted to me, that the mother of my Lord should come to me? For indeed, as soon as the voice of your greeting sounded in my ears, the babe leaped in my womb for joy. Blessed is she who believed, for there will be a fulfillment of those things which were told her from the Lord."

cross references: Gen. 22:18, Luke 11:27-28

Is Jesus your Lord? What does Lord mean?

LUKE 1:46-49

Cross references:
Ps. 138:6,
Ps. 111:9

Can you worship God for 5 things He has done for you?

And Mary said: "My soul magnifies the Lord, And my spirit has rejoiced in God my Savior. For He has regarded the lowly state of His maidservant; For behold, henceforth all generations will call me blessed. For He who is mighty has done great things for me, And holy is His name.

LUKE 1:49-53

And His mercy is on those who fear Him From generation to generation. He has shown strength with His arm; He has scattered the proud in the imagination of their hearts. He has put down the mighty from their thrones, And exalted the lowly. He has filled the hungry with good things, And the rich He has sent away empty.

How can God use children?

cross references:
Ps. 103:17
Prov. 9:10
Gen 11:8

16 LUKE 1:54-56

He has helped his servant Israel,
remembering to be merciful to
Abraham and his descendants
forever, just as he promised our
ancestors." Mary stayed with
Elizabeth for about three months
and then returned home.

cross references:
Gen. 17:7, Gal. 3:16

Are you a descendant of
Abraham? What does that
mean?

17

LUKE 1:57-60

Now Elizabeth's full time came for her to be delivered, and she brought forth a son. When her neighbors and relatives heard how the Lord had shown great mercy to her, they rejoiced with her. So it was, on the eighth day, that they came to circumcise the child; and they would have called him by the name of his father, Zacharias. His mother answered and said, "No; he shall be called John."

Did God know your name before you were born?

Cross references:
1Sam 1:20,
Luke 1:13, 14

18

LUKE 1:61-63

But they said to her, "There is no one among your relatives who is called by this name." So they made signs to his father what he would have him called. And he asked for a writing tablet, and wrote, saying, "His name is John." So they all marveled.

Zacharias and Elizabeth prayed a long time for a child. What is something that you've been waiting on from God for a long time? Can you keep praying for that like them?

Cross reference: Luke 2:21

 **LUKE 1:64-66**

Does God know what kind of child you will be?

Immediately his mouth was opened and his tongue loosed, and he spoke, praising God. Then fear came on all who dwelt around them; and all these sayings were discussed throughout all the hill country of Judea. And all those who heard them kept them in their hearts, saying, "What kind of child will this be?" And the hand of the Lord was with him.

Cross Reference: Ezekiel 3:26-27, Exodus 4:10-12

20

LUKE 1:67-71

Now his father Zacharias was filled with the Holy Spirit, and prophesied, saying: "Blessed is the Lord God of Israel, For He has visited and redeemed His people, And has raised up a horn of salvation for us In the house of His servant David, As He spoke by the mouth of His holy prophets, Who have been since the world began, That we should be saved from our enemies And from the hand of all who hate us,

What does redeemed mean? What have you been redeemed from?

Cross reference: Acts 3:17-26

22

LUKE 1:72-75

To perform the mercy promised to our fathers and to remember His holy covenant, The oath which He swore to our father Abraham: To grant us that we, Being delivered from the hand of our enemies, Might serve Him without fear, In holiness and righteousness before Him all the days of our life.

Cross references:
Gen. 22:16-18
Rom 6:18 Heb. 2:15

What have you been delivered from?

LUKE 1:76-80

22

"And you, child, will be called the prophet of the Highest; For you will go before the face of the Lord to prepare His ways, To give knowledge of salvation to His people By the remission of their sins, Through the tender mercy of our God, With which the Dayspring from on high has visited us; To give light to those who sit in darkness and the shadow of death, To guide our feet into the way of peace." So the child grew and became strong in spirit, and was in the deserts till the day of his manifestation to Israel.

How did John "prepare the way of the Lord," and how can you do the same?

Cross references:
Is. 40:3-5, Matt 3:1-3, Malachi 3:1, Ps. 107:10-11, Is. 9:2

LUKE 2:1-6

Bethlehem

And it came to pass in those days that a decree went out from Caesar Augustus that all the world should be registered. This census first took place while Quirinius was governing Syria. So all went to be registered, everyone to his own city. Joseph also went up from Galilee, out of the city of Nazareth, into Judea, to the city of David, which is called Bethlehem, because he was of the house and lineage of David, to be registered with Mary, his betrothed wife, who was with child. So it was that while they were there, the days were completed for her to be delivered.

Cross references:
Micah 5:2
Matt. 1:16

Do you know that you belong to the household of God?

24

LUKE 2:7-14

Why is Jesus more special than presents?

And she brought forth her firstborn Son, and wrapped Him in swaddling cloths, and laid Him in a manger, because there was no room for them in the inn. Now there were in the same country shepherds living out in the fields, keeping watch over their flock by night. And behold, an angel of the Lord stood before them, and the glory of the Lord shone around them, and they were greatly afraid. Then the angel said to them, "Do not be afraid, for behold, I bring you good tidings of great joy which will be to all people. For there is born to you this day in the city of David a Savior, who is Christ the Lord. And this will be the sign to you: You will find a Babe wrapped in swaddling cloths, lying in a manger." And suddenly there was with the angel a multitude of the heavenly host praising God and saying: "Glory to God in the highest, And on earth peace, goodwill toward men!"

cross references:
Ps. 148:2,
Dan. 7:10,
Rev. 5:11

25

LUKE 2:15-20

So it was, when the angels had gone away from them into heaven, that the shepherds said to one another, "Let us now go to Bethlehem and see this thing that has come to pass, which the Lord has made known to us." And they came with haste and found Mary and Joseph, and the Babe lying in a manger. Now when they had seen Him, they made widely known the saying which was told them concerning this Child. And all those who heard it marveled at those things which were told them by the shepherds. But Mary kept all these things and pondered them in her heart. Then the shepherds returned, glorifying and praising God for all the things that they had heard and seen, as it was told them.

How can you make Jesus widely known like the shepherds?

Cross references: Luke 8:39, Luke 19:37-38, Matt. 28:19

Made in the USA
Middletown, DE
20 November 2024

65087433R00015